Junaid Javaid

Simple Tech´s Approach to Human Resource Development (HRD)

GRIN Verlag

Bibliografische Information der Deutschen Nationalbibliothek:

Die Deutsche Bibliothek verzeichnet diese Publikation in der Deutschen National-
bibliografie; detaillierte bibliografische Daten sind im Internet über http://dnb.d-
nb.de/ abrufbar.

Imprint:

Copyright © 2013 GRIN Verlag GmbH
Druck und Bindung: Books on Demand GmbH, Norderstedt Germany
ISBN: 978-3-656-74822-9

This book at GRIN:

http://www.grin.com/en/e-book/281273/simple-tech-s-approach-to-human-resource-
development-hrd

GRIN - Your knowledge has value

Der GRIN Verlag publiziert seit 1998 wissenschaftliche Arbeiten von Studenten, Hochschullehrern und anderen Akademikern als eBook und gedrucktes Buch. Die Verlagswebsite www.grin.com ist die ideale Plattform zur Veröffentlichung von Hausarbeiten, Abschlussarbeiten, wissenschaftlichen Aufsätzen, Dissertationen und Fachbüchern.

Visit us on the internet:

http://www.grin.com/

http://www.facebook.com/grincom

http://www.twitter.com/grin_com

SIMPLE TECH'S APPROACH TO HRD

ASSESSMENT-1: CASE STUDY ASSIGNMENT

SHR032-6: HUMAN RESOURCE DEVELOPMENT

WRITTEN & SUBMITTED BY:

JUNAID JAVAID

COURSE TITLE:

MSc HUMAN RESOURCE MANAGEMENT

1. Introduction

This report is related to the unit of Human Resource Development (HRD). This report is focused more on the case of Simple Tech in regard to implementation HRD practices within the company. The scope of this report is broad as it would not only highlight main issues that have been faced by the company but also incorporates certain solutions for the given problems. Moreover, this report have two major sections: the first sector is based on the critical analysis of Simple Tech's approach to HRD and the second sector is emphasised on several changes in association with the company's existing approach to HRD so that it would permit the company to get maximum out of its approach to Human Resource Development.

2. Critical Analysis of Simple Tech's Current Approach to Human Resource Development (HRD)

2.1. Company Profile

Simple Tech is famous electronic manufacturing company which has been located in UK's East Midlands region. The company has employed about 700 individuals and is considered as major employer in the whole region. Moreover, the company is an entirely owned subsidiary of Japanese Multinational Corporation and that is the reason why the company all time must have to conform its corporate procedures and policies to several aspects (Strategic Planning, Implicating Corporate Values and Budgeting) of its parent company.

2.2. Objectives of HRD

It has been inclined to be essential for the organisation to have brief objective in regard to its function of HRD (Gibb, 2011). It intends organisation in the designing of effective instruction and also determined to be useful for development of HRD evaluation framework. Additionally it also direct the learner that what the organization is expecting from him/her to accomplish at the end of HRD intervention. Generally, HRD objectives can be classified into three categories:

a) **Cognitive Domain:** Objectives which are based on the acquisition of specified knowledge or information (Bloom, 1965). For example: it includes the awareness about all regulations regarding performing all tasks in a given job.

b) **Psychomotor Domain:** Objectives in the given domain are related to be demonstration of skills acquired through the specified learning & development activities (Jansma, 1999).

c) **Affective Domain:** Objectives in this domain are more concerned towards employees' values, attitudes and emotions (McCoach, Gable, & Madura, 2013). For example it involves the employees' training about keeping specified attitude towards their customers.

In relation to HRD objectives, it has been observed that Simple Tech HRD objectives are more concerned about corporate values which designed on the commitment of developing skills in all employees working as all management level. It has been discovered that Simple Tech's HRD objectives fall in the category of affective domain. Therefore, Simple Tech named such objectives as Simple Way which is focused on organisation's integrity and honesty in dealing with all of company's stakeholders (suppliers, customers, employees and local community).

2.3. Responsibility of Designing & Delivering HRD Function

Within the organization, there are various personnel which are responsible for the designing and delivery of HRD function (Phillips, 2012). In this regard there are three different roles which are significant for this purpose which are outlined below:

1) **Head of HRD Function:** It has been observed that every large organization has a Head of HRD function which are inclined to be responsible for the identification and organisation of training program or initiatives for the company's existing and new employees (Swart, Mann, Brown, & Price, 2005).

2) **HRD Consultants:** HRD Consultants are usually individuals who are specialised trainers and are responsible for the implementation of learning and development programs designed by organisation's Head of HRD Function (Ulrich, 1998).

3) **The Line Manager:** Sometime company's Line Managers could also play crucial role in the process of employees' learning and development. Line Managers within HRD function are determined to be responsible for the identification of training needs and also allocates funds & flexibility for arranging training for subordinates (Phillips & Holton, 1997).

With respect to the designing and delivery of HRD function, it has been analysed that Simple Tech has appointed HRD Head and three HRD consultants who are responsible for the designing and delivery of in house courses and also organising & managing corporate programmes' nominations. Furthermore each HRD Consultant directs different business units of Simple Tech but share the HRD interventions design and delivery across all parts of organisation once the training needs are identified.

2.4. Internal (in-House) vs. External Interventions

It has been seen that the major decision which the organization made regarding HRD interventions is whether to conduct learning & training program within or outside organisation (Sambrook & Stewart, 2013). Furthermore, cost is considered to be an important aspect while making this decision. It is also significant to understand the influence of HRD in regard to make this intervention decision. A Higher Education program is probably ascertain to be more effective if it is offered by any college or university instead of conducted within an organization (Wilson, 2005). Correspondingly if the training program is more focused on knowledge transfer or theoretical content then it may be a good option for the organization to contact external training provider (Krishnaveni, 2007).

In relation to Simple Tech case study, it has been discovered that HRD interventions within the organisation are provided in the form of one off the Job training session or short courses that are based on the needs (certain area where company's managers think that there is something which requires to be developed) identified through the company's performance management system. Additionally, Simple Tech also has an access to corporate which is usually organised by Simple Tech's parent multinational company especially for the development of staff member working in management and engineering department and this program is designed and delivered the partnership contract with leading universities around the globe.

2.5. Methods for Learning & Training Development

For the purpose of arranging HRD effort, it has been determined that organisations normally have three options. All of these options are listed and described below:

I. **On the Job Training:** Through this option, trainees got an opportunity to learn while working. This training method is seemed to be useful for jobs where it is fundamental to acquire job related information in order to enhance efficiency and effectiveness (Frazis & Loewenstein, 2007). Only negative aspect of this method is that it does not allow enough time for the trainees to learn something new. In this category, some of the common methods are: Mentoring, Job Rotation and E-learning (Rothwell & Kazanas, 2004).

II. **Off the Job Training:** This training method demanded from employees to learn new things while staying away from the workplace (Jacobs, 2003). This training sometime intends employee to spend some interval time on specified training program on frequent basis or to go enroll in a full time training course for some months (Jacobs & Phillips, 2002). Some of the methods in this category are: Training Courses, Interactive Learning and Case Studies.

III. **Blended Learning:** It has been determined that both training options discussed previously have its advantages and disadvantages. These aspects sometime resulted in arising complication or conflict which thus create mismatching among employees and employers interest (Allan, 2007), for example: an employee desires for off the Job training option for learning purposes but the employer is unwilling to release employee from the routine job duties for undergoing training program. So, in order to create perfect match between employees' and employers' needs researchers came up with this new option and termed it as Blended learning (Mantyla, 2001). This learning option combines the attributes of both training options and thus offers flexibility for both employees and employers.

In relation to the Simple Tech case study, it has been found out that the company is only intended upon off the Job Training option and provides such option in the form of one off- training session or of short courses. In addition to this aspect, the company also provides chance to the employees employed in management and engineering department to go to renowned universities across the world for acquiring knowledge and information associated with their role.

3. Recommendations

Although Simple Tech's current HRD functions and HRD interventions are seemed to be in a good shape but it has been believed that in order to strengthen its positive aspects and also to offset its weaknesses the company needed to follow some of the recommendations mentioned below:

3.1. Changes in HRD Function

3.1.1. Objectives of Company's HRD

Currently the Simple Tech's HRD objective is only based on affective domain but for evaluation and implementation purposes, the company must need to formulate new HRD objectives which also incorporates Cognitive and Psychomotor Domains along with the Affective Domain so that it would give a company better idea about its employees' learning and training development needs and accomplishments.

3.1.2. Responsibility of Designing and Delivery HRD Function

At the moment for this purpose, Simple Tech has Head of HRD and three HRD consultants. The company should look for the ways to allocate these responsibility to its Line Managers as well so that they would get a chance to share their opinion aligned with this factor and also useful to the company in relation to the designing and delivery of adequate training to existing and potential employees. And in this manner it would make positive impact on company's production quality and performance standard which could also be useful in keeping their employees' satisfied and motivated with their roles and responsibilities. But for this purpose, the company should need to hire three new Line Managers so that existing Line Managers would spend more time HRD consultants in the formulation and implementation of training and learning development programmes for new and existing Simple Tech's employees.

3.2. Changes in HRD Interventions

3.2.1. Internal (in-House) vs. External Interventions

In this category, Simple Tech only needed to increase the intensity of both interventions so that it would direct the trainers as well as trainees to achieve for the reasons of which these interventions have been designed and implicated. Additionally in regard to external interventions, Simple Tech needs to include all departments within the category of getting chance of seeking training courses designed and delivered by universities worldwide.

3.2.2. Methods for Learning & Training Development

In this category, it has been inclined that Simple Tech is only emphasised on designing and delivering off the job training which does not seems to be adequate enough for its existing as well as for new employees. So the company should also need to focus upon on the job training option. In this regard, company should prefer to adopt two on the job training methods which are defined below:

- **Mentoring:** It would be offered by company's experienced line managers to their subordinates or relatively newer employees so that they would be able to make them capable for existing role or for potential promotion (Stromei, 2001; Werner & DeSimone, 2011). One factor which need to be carefully analysed by Simple Tech in the respective manner is the successful implementation of systematic process which would make possible the transfer of skills and knowledge.

- **Job Rotation:** Simple Tech should need to rotate employees among different roles so that the employees would develop the skill of carrying out cross functional activities. So, in this way it would also reduce the company's direct labour cost.

On the other side, Simple Tech should need to keep itself away from the induction of Blended Learning for the purpose of employees' learning and development as it has been believed that the implication of this training option would add more complications and also may results in increasing the cost associated with employees' training & learning development programme.

3.3. Implementation (Action) Plan

Implementation Plan for Proposed Changes
January
<ul><li>Recruiting 3 more Front Line Managers on Part-time basis.</li><li>Formulate HRD objectives which incorporates the features of all domains (Cognitive, Psychomotor and Affective).</li></ul>
February
<ul><li>Designing the delivery plans for HRD Functions and HRD Interventions.</li><li>On the basis of formulated HRD Interventions, look for the possibility of making collaboration with renowned UK's university for the delivering off the job training courses so that it would enhance skills and knowledge of employees working apart from Management and Engineering Department.</li></ul>
May
<ul><li>Induce on the job training methods within all departments of company.</li></ul>
June
<ul><li>Alternate company's existing Performance Management System in order to enable this system to evaluate the performance of all employees as an outcome of both on the job and off the job training methods.</li></ul>
August
<ul><li>Appraise employees' performance through new Performance Management System.</li></ul>
September
<ul><li>Generate a list of aspects which must be focused for the initiation of future training sessions.</li></ul>
November
<ul><li>Conduct costs and benefits analysis of all implemented HRD functions & inventions.</li></ul>
December
<ul><li>Give briefing to company's CEO on all accomplishments of HRD Interventions.</li></ul>

Table 1 Cost Table for Proposed Changes in HRD Functions & Interventions

All proposed Changes	Cost in Pounds Sterling
• Recruitment of 3 Front Line Managers on Part-time basis	£50,000
• Contacting local universities for the delivery of off the job training courses	£10,000
• Initiating on the Job training methods (mentoring & job rotation) within an enterprise	£5,000
• Making Changes in company's existing Performance Management System	£5,000
• Appraise all Employees' Performance in response of new HRD Functions and HRD Interventions	£7,000
Total Cost	**£77,000**

Table 2 Gantt Chart for Proposed Action Plan

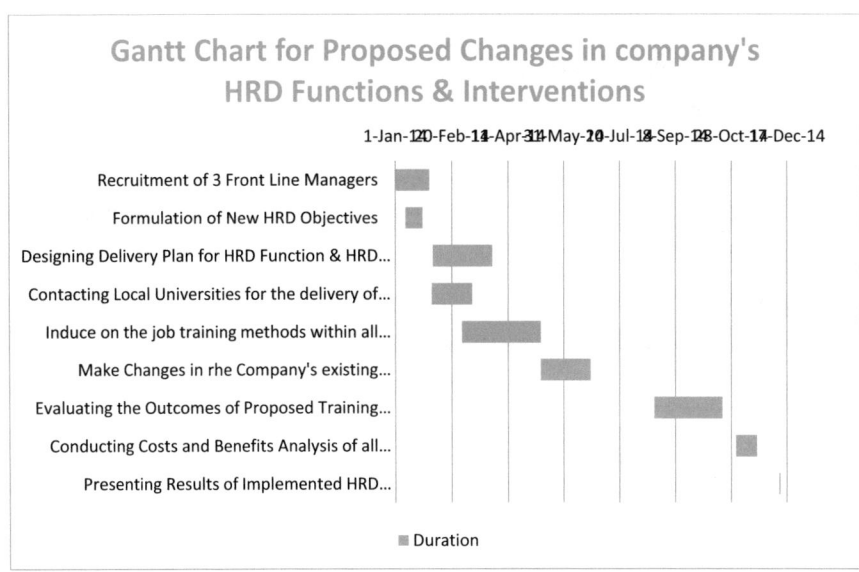

4. References

Allan, B. (2007). *Blended learning: tools for teaching and training.* Michigan: Facet.

Bloom, B. (1965). *Taxonomy of Educational Objectives: The Classification of Educational Goals.* New York: David McKay Company, Inc.

Frazis, H., & Loewenstein, M. (2007). *On-the-job Training.* Hanover: Now Publishers Inc.

Gibb, D. (2011). *Human Resource Development.* Edinburgh : Edinburgh Business School.

Jacobs, R. (2003). *Structured On-the-Job Training: Unleashing Employee Expertise in the Workplace.* San Francisco: Berrett-Koehler Publishers.

Jacobs, R., & Phillips, J. (2002). *Implementing On-the-job Learning: Thirteen Case Studies from the Real World of Training.* New York: American Society for Training and Development.

Jansma, P. (1999). *Psychomotor Domain Training and Serious Disabilities.* Oxford: University Press of America.

Krishnaveni, R. (2007). *Human Resource Development.* New Delhi: Excel Books India.

Mantyla, K. (2001). *Blending E-Learning.* New York: American Society for Training and Development.

McCoach, D., Gable, R., & Madura, J. (2013). *Instrument Development in the Affective Domain: School and Corporate Applications.* London: Springer.

Phillips, J. J. (2012). *HRD Trends Worldwide.* Houston: Routledge.

Phillips, J., & Holton, E. (1997). *Leading Organizational Change.* New York: American Society for Training and Development.

Rothwell, W., & Kazanas, H. (2004). *Improving On-the-Job Training: How to Establish and Operate a Comprehensive OJT Program.* New York: John Wiley & Sons.

Sambrook, S., & Stewart, J. (2013). *Human Resource Development in the Public Sector: The Case of Health and Social Care.* London: Routledge.

Stromei, L. K. (2001). *Creating Mentoring and Coaching Programs: Twelve Case Studies from the Real World of Training.* New York: American Society for Training and Development.

Swart, J., Mann, C., Brown, S., & Price, A. (2005). *Human Resource Development.* Oxford: Routledge.

Ulrich, D. (1998). *Delivering Results: A New Mandate for Human Resource Professional.* Boston: Harvard Business Press.

Werner, J., & DeSimone, R. (2011). *Human Resource Development.* Mason: Cengage Learning.

Wilson, J. P. (2005). *Human Resource Development: Learning & Training for Individuals & Organizatio.* London: Kogan Page Publishers.